MAKE THE RIGHT CALL

By Drew Bledsoe

with Greg Brown

Illustrations by Doug Keith

Taylor Publishing
Dallas, Texas

Greg Brown has been involved in sports for thirty years as an athlete and award-winning sportswriter. Brown started his Positively For Kids series after he was unable to find sports books for his own children that taught life lessons. Drew's book is the 15th in the series. Brown regularly speaks at schools and can be reached at greg@PositivelyForKids.com. He lives in Bothell, Washington, with his wife, Stacy, and two children, Lauren and Benji.

Doug Keith has provided illustrations for national magazines such as *Sports Illustrated for Kids*, greeting cards, and books. Keith can be reached at his internet address: atozdk@aol.com.

Being a parent can be scary. In 1996, we created the Drew Bledsoe Foundation (www.DrewBledsoe.com). Its sole purpose is to help people be better parents.

Our hope is the material on our website and the 9-part video series, called Parenting with Dignity, *will provide useful tools for families.*
1(800) 811-7949

Published by Taylor Publishing Company
1550 West Mockingbird Lane
Dallas, Texas 75235

Designed by
David Timmons

Library of Congress Cataloging-in-Publication Data

Bledsoe, Drew, 1972–
    Make the right call / by Drew Bledsoe with Greg Brown.
        p.   cm.
    Summary: Examines the life of the New England Patriots quarterback who led the team to the Super Bowl in 1997, discussing the steps he has taken to try to make good decisions.
    ISBN 0-87833-215-4
    1. Bledsoe, Drew, 1972–   —Juvenile literature. 2. Football players—United States—Biography—Juvenile literature. 3. New England Patriots (Football team)—Juvenile literature.
[1. Bledsoe, Drew, 1972– . 2. Football players.]
I. Brown, Greg. II. Title.
GV939.B56A3   1998
796.332'092—dc21
[B]   98-38629
                                          CIP
                                          AC

Printed in the United States of America
10 9 8 7 6 5 4 3 2 1

Drew at age 10

Hi! I'm Drew Bledsoe.

I grew up around the game of football because my dad was a high school football coach. Even as a 10-year-old I had dreams of playing the game.

But it wasn't until the seventh grade that I made the decision to try to play quarterback.

It was an odd choice at the time. A growth spurt left me gangly and uncoordinated for my first season of organized football. I wasn't the best passer on our team—in fact, I could barely throw a spiral—so the coach suggested I try another position. I played tight end that entire season. Still, I worked on passing by staying after practice to throw.

I was determined to be a quarterback. I wrote my goal on paper. Then I made decisions that gave me the best chance of achieving what I wanted.

Now that I'm an NFL quarterback for the New England Patriots, I've written this book to help you be a good decision maker too.

Whether or not you succeed in life mostly depends on the decisions you make.

We all make hundreds of choices every day—what to eat, what to wear, what to do, what to say. Those daily choices eventually define who we are.

In football, players must make split-second decisions on the field. As quarterback, the outcome of the game often rests on the decisions I make. What play should I call? Should I pass the football? To whom should I throw it?

Every football play is designed to score a touchdown. The problem is that defensive players are running around trying to stop us. And sometimes people miss their blocks or players drop the ball or quarterbacks miss their mark and throw interceptions. I've certainly thrown my share of both touchdowns and interceptions.

"Successful people know that failure is not an end, it's a beginning."

So nobody makes the right call all the time. The decisions of others affect me, but long ago my parents taught me that my decisions are the only ones I can control.

Knowing you made the right choice is a great feeling. In football, there's a magical moment when I realize I've made the right call to score a touchdown.

Even before I throw, I smile and know, "Yeah, we've got 'em." And when it all works, it brings elation and pride in knowing, as a team, we did it right.

My parents saw our family as a team—the Bledsoes vs. the World. They understood that just as coaches can't make the plays on the field, parents can't live their children's lives. So they believed their number one job as parents was to teach my brother and me how to make good choices.

Throughout this book I will tell you my true-life stories of decisions I've made. My hope is that after you read this book you will better understand the process of decision making.

Also, I want to share some of the parenting techniques Mom and Dad used with me so that your family can prepare you to make life choices.

Drew and his great-grandfather.

Along the bottom of these pages you will see special sayings. My father compiled these from letters his grandfather wrote him. Four-star Navy Admiral Albert McQueen Bledsoe collected about 200 famous quotes. He wrote them in the margins of letters to my dad. You can read them and think about them as you go through my story or come back to them later. We call them "Bledsoe's Wisdom."

My parents were raised in Ellensburg, a small windswept town in the middle of Washington state.

Mac, my dad, was raised on a cattle ranch and dreamed of being a cowboy, playing football for the University of Washington Huskies, and becoming a teacher and coach.

Barbara, my mom, grew up on a dairy farm with interests of being a cowgirl, cheerleader, and school teacher.

They dated on and off from junior high through college and fulfilled their dreams.

Dad earned a spot on the UW football team as an offensive tackle and became a team captain. He played professional football three seasons with the old Continental League.

My parents married the summer before their senior year in college, and both graduated with teaching degrees.

"We grow in the images of those we love."

Dad used positive reinforcement on one rat by giving it food each time it moved to the ball, then each time it touched it, and finally for every "shot" it made in the hoop. Waiting to reward the rat took months of patience.

The second rat got negative reinforcement. It received electric shocks for wrong moves. That rat quickly learned how to make a basket within days.

After the study, however, Dad noticed that the shocked rat never touched the ball again. The first continued to make baskets, seemingly with joy, even without rewards.

Dad concluded that positive learning is more effective in the long run. That idea became the foundation of his ideas about how to be an effective teacher and parent.

While in college, Dad studied psychology, the science of behavior. As a class project, he set out to teach rats how to "play basketball."

Actually, he wanted to teach two rats to put a Ping-Pong ball through a hoop made from a coat hanger.

Fellow students laughed, saying it couldn't be done. But he did it!

Another idea that stuck with my parents was delivered by Dr. Jim Cobb.

On February 14, 1972, a few minutes after my birth, Dr. Cobb placed me in my parents' loving arms and said, "I want you to remember something: this child is not yours. He is on loan to you for 18 years. He already has a will of his own."

The thought that a child is not a possession, but an independent individual, influenced how they raised me from the beginning.

"Accept me as I am so I may learn what I can."

An early decision made by my parents was to invest time in a family instead of a house.

Mom postponed her teaching career to be a stay-at-home mother. To do that on one income, we lived in an old mobile home, affectionately called "The Gray Whale," until I was 4 years old.

At first, they wanted to shelter me by living on an isolated dirt road with no television or negative influences.

That plan changed two years later when I pretended to shoot a

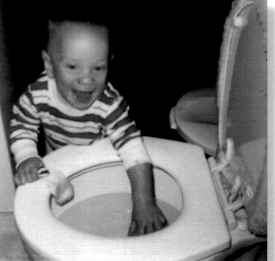

Exploring new things and playing in the toilet were favorite pastimes.

playmate with my finger and thumb shaped like a gun.

That's when my parents knew it made more sense to prepare me for the world rather than hide me from it.

While Mom nurtured me 24 hours a day, Dad was off teaching and coaching at a high school.

Even with those outside demands, Dad found time to spend with me.

He read to me at night. We laughed playing sports or games together. And we built things, such as models or remote-controlled cars.

Every Halloween Dad and I made a production of making my costume. One year I was a robot. Another year we turned my bike into a moving sailboat.

Both Mom and Dad proudly attended my school functions and my athletic events.

My parents were wise enough to know that it's not the quality of time, it's the amount of time parents spend with their children that counts the most.

"Quiet moments are life's rewards."

There are many ways my parents express their love and support. One is through family traditions.

Ever since my first birthday, Dad has decorated my birthday cake. It was exciting to see what Dad would create. The "Chopper Cake," which looked like a motorcycle, was a favorite. The year I signed to play at Washington State, Dad made the cake look like a WSU helmet.

When I turned 22, Dad thought I had outgrown his cakes, so he didn't decorate one. I did miss it, and jokingly lamented, "Dad didn't even make me a cake this year."

DREW,
WERE SO PROUD OF OUR OLDEST SON. YOU ARE RAPIDLY BECOMING A VERY FINE YOUNG MAN. YOU CAN ALWAYS COUNT ON ONE THING IN THIS WORLD...
YOUR MOTHER AND FATHER WILL ALWAYS LOVE YOU!
LOVE MOM & DAD

After hearing that, Dad went to the store and bought a sheet cake and frosting to keep our cake tradition alive.

One of the many special things Mom has done is write me letters. Sometimes they were notes of encouragement I found in my lunch. Other times they recorded her feelings during important moments in my life.

At the time I took them for granted as just another note from Mom. But I saved most of them, and now it's great to have that family history. Mom's nickname for me used to be, and still is, "Biggie."

Messages of love from my parents

1. They repeatedly told me they loved me unconditionally.
2. They put their unconditional love in writing.
3. We made things together.
4. We played games together.
5. They watched my games and school activities.
6. They listened to me.
7. They gave me hugs.
8. They let me express my opinions.
9. They defined the meanings of family, home, and love.
10. They taught me the language of love.

"There are two lasting gifts we can give our children—one is roots, the other is wings."

11

Grandpa Stew learned it was OK for men to say, "I love you." He said it to us kids often and was quick to give us hugs.

I don't remember the first time my parents told me they loved me. That's because I have heard it constantly since my birth.

Dad, however, didn't hear those words from his father, or even get a hug, until he was 36 years old. It caused him years of pain.

Grandpa Stew was a hardworking rancher, a rough guy with a loving heart. He was a leader, first as a World War II fighter pilot and later as the Washington State Speaker of the House. But he came from a generation of fathers who were expected to be tough, not tender. When Dad misbehaved as a child, he received an old-fashioned belt whipping.

Dad decided that just because he was punished that way didn't make it right. Dad and Mom never hit or spanked us.

The night Dad and Grandpa Stew made things right happened after a high school homecoming football game Dad had coached. Before the game players ran onto the field with their parents. Dad, who was the head coach, ran out wishing his parents were with him.

As it turned out, they were in the stands. Dad didn't know they were there until after the game. Dad and Grandpa Stew talked afterward, and Dad said how he wished his father had been on the field with him.

Then Dad told his father how much he loved him and thanked him for all the ways he had shown love without saying it.

With tears streaming down his face, Grandpa Stew gave my Dad a bear hug and said, "You are the sun that lights my days and the moon that lights my nights. I love you, son."

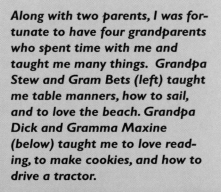

Along with two parents, I was fortunate to have four grandparents who spent time with me and taught me many things. Grandpa Stew and Gram Bets (left) taught me table manners, how to sail, and to love the beach. Grandpa Dick and Gramma Maxine (below) taught me to love reading, to make cookies, and how to drive a tractor.

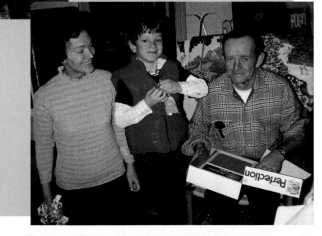

"Everything that grows changes."

A football game helped heal Dad's relationship with his father, and the sport has also produced a strong bond between my father and me.

Dad co-founded the All-Northwest Football Camp. I attended my first summer football camp at age 1½, when I was barely taller than a T-shirt. NFL players were guest instructors.

That year I met legendary Oakland Raiders receiver Fred Biletnikoff. I'm told I made a great first impression by relieving myself into a pair of his empty shoes that were sitting on the grass. He forgave me, but he still teases me about it.

Summer after summer I attended the camp with Dad. It gave me the opportunity to focus on football and meet professional players one-on-one. I got to see them as real, down-to-earth people. It was enlightening to see guys who had achieved success and were still friendly, charitable, nice people.

Fred Biletnikoff (left) poses with Drew in these two camp pictures. The top photo shows New England's last two first-pick quarterbacks—Jim Plunckett (right) and Drew (in the striped shirt). The bottom photo is of Fred and Drew with camp leaders 20 years later.

I've never gotten over my biggest childhood fear. I'm afraid of snakes. Looking at a snake gives me the chills. It's my one phobia.

Being around the game so much allowed me to soak up information. After elementary school in the fall, I'd often visit Dad at high school football practice.

I looked up to the high school guys as if they were professionals.

I'd help with equipment or be the water boy. It didn't matter. I just enjoyed hanging around the team. I'd poke my head into practice to learn the plays, coverages, and strategies.

One day in second grade, I threw a football to move it aside during a practice. One of the senior players saw me throw it and said, "Hey coach, your kid has a good arm. Maybe he'll be a quarterback."

Every idea needs a seed, and perhaps that day one was planted.

"To imagine is everything."

Because of Dad's coaching, we moved five times before I finished elementary school. Leaving friends was tough, but it taught me I could make new friends and that being by yourself is OK sometimes, too.

The best rule I learned about friendship is: If you want a friend, be a friend.

Playing sports always helped. Despite our moves, I did well in school.

While looking at old school work Mom saved in albums, we found two assignments that were ironic.

For one assignment I wrote about being an NFL quarterback. I was a little off on the salary.

The other was a report I did on the state of Massachusetts, where I now live.

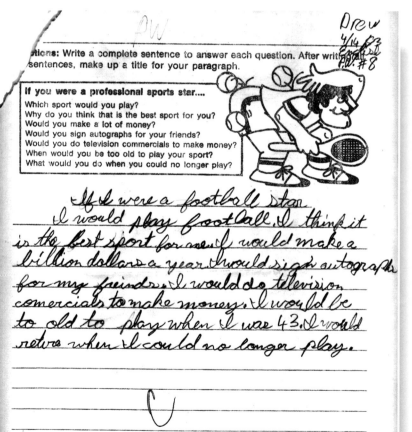

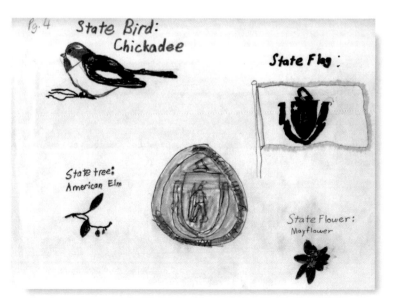

During my elementary years I wasn't the best athlete in school. One thing I did have, however, was endurance.

I competed in the 400-meter race and won a first-place title in the grueling distance. I also swam.

I proved my stamina in third grade during a bike-a-thon in Waterville, Washington, to raise money for charity.

I rode my bike around and around the course. After each lap a tag would be placed on our handle bars. As my tag collection grew, other riders dropped out. Finally, I was the last one riding. I kept going and going. Organizers finally stopped me because they wanted to go home.

"The farther you reach, the farther you'll go."

As a Little League pitcher I had endurance and a blazing fastball, but not much control. Hitters were afraid to face me because I often hit batters. Sometimes I accidentally hit friends of mine who were on other teams.

My first memorable sports moment came on the basketball court in sixth grade during a game for the city championship. I was fouled with only seconds left on the clock and the score tied. I calmly made two free throws for the victory.

Surprisingly, that pressure situation didn't make me nervous. I somehow found a way to focus despite the pressure. I have never feared having

the outcome of a game depend on me.

Dad has taught me the only thing I can do in any situation is do my best.

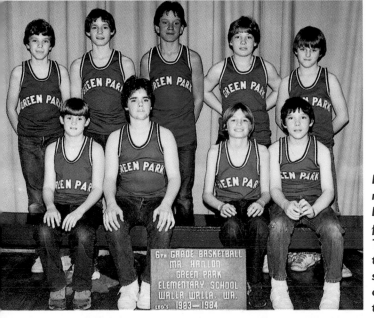

Drew (in the middle of the back row) didn't play in jeans. This picture was taken during school, and he didn't have time to put on shorts.

For some demanding coaches, trying your best is never enough. One of my most embarrassing sports experiences happened when I played Pony League baseball.

While in the outfield, I threw the ball to the wrong base, allowing a runner to score.

The coach screamed at me and immediately pulled me out of the game. I sat on the bench steaming mad.

In the final inning, the coach brought me back as the pitcher with the bases loaded and a one-run lead. That's probably the hardest I've ever thrown a baseball, because I was so angry at the coach. I struck out a couple batters for the victory.

Dad was upset with the coach

for humiliating me, but, as usual, my father never confronted my coach. Instead, Dad gave me a big hug after the game and said he was proud of how I handled myself. He added, "I don't care if you throw strikes or balls, I still love you."

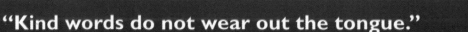

"Kind words do not wear out the tongue."

None of the places we lived when I was in elementary school offered youth football, so my first experience playing the sport came in seventh grade in Walla Walla, Washington.

Being around Dad's teams, I knew I wanted to play quarterback. However, after my first few junior high practices it was clear that my friend Tommy Knecht was the better quarterback.

My coach pulled me aside and said I should try another position, such as tight end. He explained what I already knew: I was too slow, I couldn't throw very far, and my throws weren't accurate.

That night I told Dad what happened, expecting he would call the coach and ask him to give me another chance.

Dad simply said, "It sounds like you know the things you need to work on." He added that I shouldn't let others rob my dreams.

I played tight end that season and actually enjoyed the position. Still, I held on to my dream. After practice I'd play catch to work on my throwing.

Tommy moved away that year, so I got my chance to play quarterback in eighth grade and have played there ever since.

By the ninth grade I started working out seriously for football. I'd play catch with my friend Andy Jamison before school and during the summer.

Our commitment to working out with each other lasted throughout high school. We motivated each other. When one of us didn't feel like practicing, he would be convinced by the other to work out.

If it weren't for Andy, who knows if I would have become the quarterback I am today.

Many times my brother, Adam, who is six years younger and is my only sibling, would tag along to our private practices. As with most younger brothers, Adam was always in my shadow seeking attention.

Drew and Adam at football camp.

"Good habits are as easily formed as bad ones."

Many times I saw Adam as irritating. He had a knack for doing things that bugged me. Even his breathing bothered me sometimes. One time he "accidentally" tripped on the power cord to our word processor and erased my entire school report.

During car trips we'd get on each other's nerves. Mom and Dad would stop the car. But instead of separating us, they would talk to us individually about ways we could get along. I'd agree to play cards or a game with Adam. He agreed to not bother me as much.

We weren't perfect, though.

Sometimes we were sent to our rooms as punishment for misbehaving. I remember being grounded in my room, thinking about how much I hated my family and how I just wanted to grow up and leave home. I think all kids have those feelings. But those feelings never lasted long for me.

Sometimes, out of frustration, I'd throw verbal darts at Adam with put-down humor. When Mom overheard it, she helped me realize how much Adam looked up to me and that I had a responsibility as the older brother to set a good example.

Drew gives his brother and his friend Kristi a ride on a snowmobile.

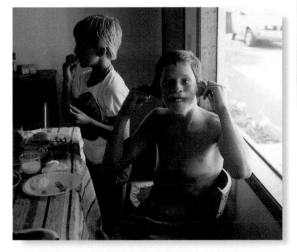

Responsibility and honesty are concepts my parents made sure we learned. My parents had unique ways of teaching us.

Growing tired of washing mountains of dirty towels, my parents sat us down one day when I was 14 and Adam was 8. They gave me two red towels and Adam two blue towels. They explained what they wanted. We were to use the two towels for a whole week, and only then would they be washed.

Sure enough, the first two towels ended up on our bedroom floor after we showered. So did the second two the next day. On the third day all four towels were still wet, piled on our floor, when we got out of the shower. We begged, but my parents made us use our cold, soggy towels.

We figured out in a hurry that if we hung up our towel we'd have a dry one the next day.

My parents also gave us examples of acting responsibly and honestly by respecting the laws of the land, both written and unwritten.

One day Dad and I went to the grocery store. The cashier gave him his change, and we walked out. In the parking lot, Dad noticed he was given a $20 instead of a $10 bill. After explaining to me what happened, he turned around and gave back the extra change. The cashier was very thankful, because the mistake would have come out of her pay.

Several weeks later, Dad and I were in the same store with the same cashier. Dad explained that he had forgotten his checkbook and didn't have any money. The cashier remembered Dad's honesty and gave him the money solely on his promise to repay it.

"He that loses his honesty has nothing left to lose."

My most lasting lesson on honesty and responsibility came in the third grade.

A friend and I were playing in a grass field close to my house, and we decided to burn an ant hill. The entire field, about the size of a city block, quickly became ablaze.

I ran home and Mom called the fire department, which put out the fire before the flames damaged anyone's property.

When Dad asked us who started the fire, my friend and I pointed at each other and said, "He did it!"

With Dad's permission, the sheriff hauled us down to the police station and lectured us. I remember seeing a jail cell and the chief pointing to it and saying, "That's where you'll end up if you keep playing with fire." That frightened me so much I didn't touch a match for months. The first time I lit our fireplace was a big deal.

I decided on my own punishment. I wrote a letter of apology to every fireman who responded to the fire and hand-delivered them to each person.

Dear Doc Hill,
I am truly sorry for starting that fire Friday. I learned a lesson from what I did. I know that I risked my health and safety and the safety of others by what I did. I hope you and the other firemen will forgive me. I am thankful that you me were there to prevent my carelessness from hurting someone.

Sincerely
Drew Bledsoe

Drew gives his cousin Erin a ride on his motorcycle.

I made some other poor decisions that got me in trouble as a kid, but the fire was the biggest. Still, my parents gave us the freedom to prove ourselves.

When I was 12, all I wanted in the world was a motorcycle. I worked mowing lawns and other odd jobs to earn money to buy it, but my parents were hesitant.

"I'm responsible. I can handle it," I told them.

They finally agreed and allowed me to get a motorcycle. I received moto-cross pads that Christmas.

I obeyed the boundaries of where I could ride and stayed off

public roads. I had many hours of fun riding the motorcycle and never injured myself or anyone else.

Then, in ninth grade, my parents showed their ultimate trust in me. They gave me a week-long ski trip as a present. They allowed me and a friend to fly by ourselves to Utah to stay with my aunt. We packed our own lunches every day and took a bus up to the ski area and skied all day on our own. Everything worked out great.

That's when I knew for sure my parents trusted me.

Drew (left) and friend Jed Barnes (middle) pose atop a Utah mountain with a new-found skiing buddy.

"The measure of a man's real character is what he would do if he knew he would never be found out."

But freedom has its risks.

My parents let me ride my skateboard and bicycle wherever I wanted, and I loved jumping off and over things with both.

In sixth grade I almost dislocated my jaw in a bicycle accident when I jumped into a ditch.

My friends and I found a 10-foot-deep ditch and decided to speed down one side so we could jet up the other side and fly into the air. I went too fast off the edge and landed in the middle of the ditch, snapping my bike in half.

I flew over the handle bars and landed on my chin. I was fortunate to walk away with cuts and bruises.

I also broke my wrist skateboarding in eighth grade when I jumped off a curb.

My most serious injury, however, came while playing in my first varsity football game.

"A ship in a harbor is safe, but that is not what ships are built for."

Drew's dad wore headsets as a coach and offensive coordinator.

Drew wore No. 12 in high school, and Andy was No. 11.

My high school football career started by sitting on the bench my first four varsity games as a sophomore. Dad was the co-head coach, and he didn't want people to think he favored his son.

So I started playing junior varsity. Halfway into the season the varsity team wasn't doing very well. The other coaches convinced Dad to give me a chance.

I started against Borah High, one of Idaho's best teams.

In the final minutes we were losing, so I dropped back to throw a desperation pass. A tackler rammed his helmet into my stomach and knocked the wind out of me. I shook off the hit and finished the game. My stomach pain continued hours after the game. I went to the hospital.

Doctors discovered the blow dangerously pushed my liver into my backbone. My liver swelled with blood and was in danger of bursting.

I missed the rest of the season. My first big chance, and I was out. I was upset for quite awhile. The injury did help me keep football in perspective.

"A group becomes a team when each member is sure enough of himself and his contribution to praise the skills of others."

Before each sport started, coaches had us sign a contract promising that we would not drink alcohol or use tobacco or illegal drugs during the season.

That promise was important to me, and I kept it. Others, including some friends, decided differently.

Although I felt left out sometimes and wasn't invited to some parties, I didn't struggle with the decision. In my mind I only had to make that decision once. My true friends respected that decision.

A group of us—both girls and guys—who decided to keep our training promise often hung out together on weekends. We found we didn't need drugs to have fun.

A favorite pastime was to go out with a video camera and make crazy movies or take pictures.

It was about that time that my parents suggested Adam and I write a Top 20 List of the things most important in our lives. This list was not for anyone else to see, and it could change as our priorities changed.

If you're wondering, football has never been higher than fourth or fifth on my list.

One priority I had was to follow the guidelines of playing sports at my high school. I played football and basketball and ran track.

Drew shines his first truck.

Drew and ninth-grade friends perform "The Super Bowl Shuffle" at a school assembly.

Drew and Snuffy, the family dog.

High school prom night.

"It takes courage to stand alone."

I kept busy during the summer driving wheat trucks, working construction, or working in Dad's wood shop. The summer before my junior year Andy Jamison and I found time to play catch for three hours a day. I also started working out at the local YMCA on old weight machines that were much too small for my growing 6-foot-4 frame.

I also trained my mind. I'd carry around notes written to myself that stated my goals as a player: "I throw three hours a day; I hustle on every play; the team always comes first; I'm the first on the field and the last to leave." The notes were personal, written in the present, and positive.

Before our first game, however, I learned that sports offer no guarantees. Andy broke his kneecap in practice and missed the entire season.

I felt terrible for him. We had worked so hard together. It wasn't fair.

It was tough on Andy, but to his credit, he still helped out with practice and cheered us on at games.

With a new coach, we finished 4–5, and I led our conference in passing. Dad was the offensive coordinator, and it was special to continue our coach-player relationship.

In basketball, I didn't make the starting lineup. Still, I enjoyed being part of the team.

And I set a school record in track by clearing 6-foot-7 in the high jump.

But football remained my favorite sport.

"The road to anywhere starts from where you are."

That next summer, our coach adopted a new passing system for my senior year.

I loved the new "spread offense" with four or five receivers, including Andy. It worked so well one game I threw for a state-record 509 yards. I didn't realize it was a record until after the game. I didn't feel like celebrating much, though, because we still lost the game.

Our team started slow but finished strong. Our 6–3 record earned us a tie-breaking game for a playoff spot. Unfortunately, we lost.

My height, passing arm, and good grades (3.67 grade point average) produced interest from hundreds of schools. I narrowed those down to four schools—Stanford, Miami, Washington, and Washington State.

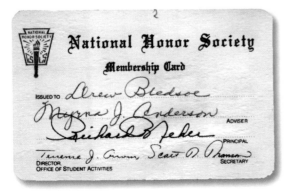

Dad never pressured me to go to his alma mater, Washington. He knew I had to decide for my own reasons.

I made a list of all the positives of each school. Then I made a list of my values and connected the two lists. Two schools offered big-time media exposure, and one pushed the money value of their degree. But fame and money weren't on my values list. Washington State ended up with the most connections between lists, plus it was close to home, and it felt right.

Drew and and his family celebrate his decision to attend WSU.

Senior Season

State Player of the Year
156 completions
272 passes
2,560 yards
25 touchdowns

Soon after arriving at WSU, however, things started feeling all wrong.

I went to WSU with self-doubts about competing at the Pac-10 level. With senior quarterback Brad Gossen and talented sophomore Aaron Garcia, who had led the Pac-10 in passing the year before, I didn't expect much playing time my freshman year.

It took me two weeks of practice to realize I could hold my own on the field. In the third game, I got my chance to play against USC.

I ran onto the field and had a dream-like experience. It wasn't until I saw myself on the gigantic L.A. Coliseum big-screen TV that I knew it was real.

I completed six of 12 passes for 145 yards and a touchdown in my debut.

That next week coach Mike Price announced that I would be the starting quarterback. That decision tore the team apart. Most players thought Brad or Aaron deserved the starting job. I found myself in the middle of a huge controversy.

Two-thirds of the WSU players refused to talk to me the rest of the season, even in the huddle.

Those were tough times. I made many late-night calls home to family and friends to vent my frustrations. During tough times it's important to talk about your feelings with others. On the field the only thing I could do was keep my mouth shut and play.

Despite their disappointment in reduced playing time, Brad and Aaron showed a lot of class by talking to me. They were both helpful and positive the whole season, in which we finished 3–8, including a humiliating 55–10 loss to cross-state rival Washington.

My sophomore year had its ups and downs. I was sacked 56 times, yet still managed to lead the Pac-10 in passing. We finished 4–7, including another big loss to Washington, 56–21.

I nap soundly for 15 minutes before going out on the field for a game. The night before a game I sleep like a rock. The night after a game I can't sleep at all.

"Do not pray for an easy life; pray to be a strong person."

WSU Highlights

Named PAC-10 Most Valuable Player
   junior season
7,373 career passing yards—ranked
   2nd on WSU's all-time list
46 career touchdowns—ranked 2nd
   on WSU's all-time list
Passed for school-record 476 yards in
   Copper Bowl victory
Threw a football 85 yards
First Freshman starter at WSU in
   more than 30 years

Drew and coach Price.

I owe a lot to WSU coach Mike Price. He taught me much about the game and how to have fun. The most valuable thing he gave me was the freedom to make mistakes. He didn't try to mold me. He allowed my strengths to shine.

Two victories highlighted my junior year.

We beat Utah 31–28 in the Copper Bowl, WSU's first bowl appearance in four years.

The sweetest win, though, was the regular-season finale when we upset No. 5-ranked Washington in the snow. The 42–23 pounding of the defending national champs remains one of my most thrilling victories.

At season's end, I faced another tough decision. Should I stay at WSU for my senior season or play in the NFL? Again, I made my two lists. This time, fulfilling my long-time dream of playing in the NFL won out.

My junior year I went on a fateful double date. My roommate invited me to play tennis with him, his girl-friend, and another girl.

Maura Healy was my date. I was immediately attracted to her fun-loving, outgoing personality. Plus she was beautiful and athletic. She defeated me soundly in our singles match. I asked for a rematch, and soon we were dating.

I didn't mind that she knew little about football and didn't know I was a quarterback.

She does now. We've been togeth-er ever since that first tennis date.

Picking a sports agent is an important decision for a professional athlete. Dad helped me compile a detailed file on three of the top agents.

I went with Leigh Steinberg not only because he's the best and most creative, but because he stresses the importance of athletes giving back to the community.

I didn't really believe I'd be the number one overall choice of the 1993 draft until the Patriots picked me. It's also hard to believe someone would pay me $14 million to play football. We figured out that's equal to 200 years of Dad's teaching salary. I know that's crazy. Dad has touched the lives of hundreds of students. I throw a football through the air.

The money has never been my motivation. In fact, the first six-figure check I received I accidentally left in my car for days. I took the car in for some work, and the repair shop called and said they found the check.

That first year in New England, I quickly learned that to whom much is given, much is expected.

"There is nothing wrong with men possessing riches. The wrong comes when the riches possess men."

First, he made me fetch things during practice for him as if I were a manager. During practice he constantly yelled at players and played mind games.

At times I wanted to scream back, but I made a decision not to. Parcells' tactics taught me to be more thick-skinned and how to play through distractions.

We all have to learn how to relate to different people. Every teacher or boss you encounter will have their own ways of doing things. You have to learn to deal with it, even when you don't agree. I dealt with it.

The Patriots had the worst record in the league the previous season. I earned the starting job in preseason, and everyone expected great things. But we lost our first four games and seven of the next eight.

After a loss to Pittsburgh, in which I threw five interceptions, I picked up every regional newspaper to see how bad it would be when the media was down on me.

One newspaper called my effort "the worst in Patriots' history."

I normally don't read articles about myself. In a way, it was comical. It was also a challenge. I wanted to prove them wrong.

We did by winning our final four games.

The losses were tough, almost as tough as learning to play under coach Bill Parcells' style.

Parcells really challenged me.

We started the 1994 season with high hopes, but we lost the first two games and later had a four-game losing streak. The pivotal game proved to be what is called the greatest come-from-behind win in Patriots history. We were down by 17 points at the half against Minnesota and still rallied with 53 second-half passes to win 26–20 in overtime. Even Parcells got emotional after the game and said to us, "You've given me hope. That was valiant."

We won our last seven games to make the playoffs for the first time in eight years. Even though we lost to Cleveland in my first football playoff game, we all felt the team was going in the right direction.

After the season, I returned to Walla Walla to say thank you to those who had helped me.

Friends gathered for a presentation at the same YMCA where I had lifted weights. I donated

Drew gives his mom a hug.

Drew meets kids in his hometown.

Drew passed for 4,555 yards—a team record—and 25 touchdowns and became the youngest Pro Bowl quarterback.

$110,000 to the YMCA for remodeling and new weight machines. It also gave me a chance to thank many people publicly, including my parents.

A special moment came when I gave my New England jersey to Andy Jamison, the friend who pushed me to work so hard. Andy played small college football after high school but didn't make it to the professional level. From college on I've worn No. 11, because that

was Andy's number in high school.

So when I gave him my jersey, I said, "I'm proud to wear your number in the NFL, Andy."

There wasn't a dry eye in the room, including mine.

"The smallest good deed is better than the greatest good intention."

Drew and Adam, who went on to play football at the University of Colorado.

Maura, my college sweetheart, to marry me under the stars on a camping trip, but we attended a friend's wedding in Walla Walla and started talking about marriage afterward. I decided I couldn't wait. To be alone, we went to a nearby junior high and sat on the softball field bleachers. There I asked her if she would marry me, and she said, "Yes!"

We had an engagement party a few weeks later. In front of the whole family, I said I wanted my best friend to be my best man. I walked over to the kid who used to bug me so much and said to my brother, Adam, "Well, kid, will you do it?"

Maura and I were married in Portland, Oregon, her hometown, in May of 1996 with Adam at my side.

Maura and Drew.

New Patriots owner Robert Kraft took over before the 1995 season and offered me a contract that made me the highest-paid player in NFL history.

The 1995 season fell short of our expectations as we failed to make the playoffs. An early-season shoulder separation on my non-throwing side forced me to miss a game and ended my consecutive-start streak at 23 games.

The next year proved to be Super.

I had romantic plans to ask

We began the 1996 season with two straight losses and many were expecting a repeat downfall. I wasn't playing well. My playing was tight and timid—until Dad gave me some advice.

Normally, Dad and I rarely talk about football strategy, and he never makes suggestions about what I "should be doing" on the field. He only offers advice when I ask for it. That might seem odd with him being around football so much as a player and coach, but he's never wanted football to come between our father-son relationship.

One day, however, we were talking, and I shared with him how down I felt. He said, "You play like you're not having fun. If you play so cautiously, afraid of making mistakes, you'll be just another Joe. I don't think you want to be another Joe. Go play for fun. Pull the trigger on your throws. Take a chance on losing."

Those words of encouragement made the difference.

Some people think I don't show enough emotion on the field; some think I don't get excited about wins or feel the sting of losses. That's not true. I'm just not the type to jump up and down all the time. I've always been calm and in control during games. I think that's a strength for a quarterback.

"We cannot direct the wind, but we can adjust the sail."

I started to play with confidence again, and our team came together. We won 11 of our last 14 games to claim the American Football Conference East Division title.

We beat Pittsburgh in the fog, 28–3, for New England's first home playoff victory. It was extra special for me, because Dad was on the sidelines that day—his first time on an NFL field during a game.

Our AFC Championship victory had an ironic twist as I faced Jacksonville quarterback Mark Brunell in subfreezing temperatures. Brunell was the Washington quarterback when our Cougars beat them.

Our win over the Jaguars earned us a trip to Super Bowl XXXI in New Orleans to meet red-hot Green Bay.

The Packers played almost perfectly, and we didn't. We were down 10–0 after six minutes thanks

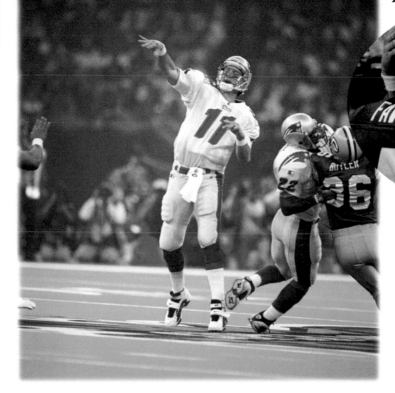

to a 54-yard Brett Favre touchdown pass and an interception that led to a field goal.

Green Bay's big plays hurt us. A record-breaking 81-yard touchdown pass by Favre made it 27–14 at the half.

I'm proud that we fought back. We made it a game at 27–21, but on the next play Packer Desmond Howard returned the kickoff 99

Drew congratulates Brett Favre after Super Bowl XXXI

yards for a score. A two-point conversion set the final score at 35–21.

A Super Bowl loss is the ultimate defeat.

You win a bunch of games in a row to make it there, and you forget what it's like to lose. To go that far and play that well and not win is hard to swallow.

To battle back and watch the kickoff return for a touchdown was really disappointing. But football is a team game. You win as a team and lose together, too.

The only thing that helped was that nobody expected us to go that far.

"Success consists of getting up just one more time than you fall."

After the Super Bowl coach Parcells left to join the New York Jets. New coach Pete Carroll brought a management style dramatically different from Parcells'.

Carroll allows players some freedom and expects players to be responsible for helping lead the team.

Key injuries hurt us during the 1997 season, but we stayed in the tight playoff race.

In the second-to-last game of the regular season, we led Pittsburgh by eight points with two minutes to play. We had the ball near midfield and just needed to run out the clock to clinch a playoff spot.

We called for a low-risk screen pass. Unfortunately, I didn't see a Pittsburgh defender who rushed in. He intercepted the pass and raced to the 18-yard line. Pittsburgh scored and added a two-point conversion to force overtime. Pittsburgh got the ball first in overtime and drove for a game-winning field goal.

It was a crushing defeat, the type that can crush confidence. It was the first time I had thrown an interception that lost a game we had locked up. For eight long days it seemed that one poor pass could cost us the season.

Playing sports, however, has taught me that when you make poor plays on the field you can't let them eat away at you. You forgive yourself, learn from it, and move on. You have to be able to put things behind you.

Fortunately, we beat Miami 14–12 the next week to make the playoffs and won the East Division title. We faced the Dolphins in the first round of the playoffs and won again, 17–3. Pittsburgh ended our season in the next round with a frustrating 7–6 loss.

For the Record

Second-youngest NFL quarterback to surpass 15,000 yards passing
Set seven New England team records in first five seasons
Fourth quarterback in history with multiple 4,000-yard seasons

"Live for today. Dream for tomorrow. Learn from yesterday."

Two things happened off the field in 1997—one, the birth of my son, marked the most joyous day in my life, the other, one of the most embarrassing.

It would be easy to skip over the latter, but I mention it so you can learn something from it.

It's a team tradition for Patriot teammates to get together one night a week. Sometimes families go out for pizza, or sometimes only players meet. It strengthens team unity.

On one of those nights, a teammate and I decided to drop by a rock concert. We were invited on stage with the band and waved to the crowd.

Sometimes at rock concerts people jump off the stage into the crowd, which catches the person with hundreds of hands.

People chanted for us to jump. It seemed harmless. Not for one second did I think I could hurt myself or someone else. For the first time in my life I listened to peer pressure.

So I did a slow-motion fall into the crowd. The sea of hands caught me. I floated above the crowd until they gently let me down.

Later, news broke that someone in the crowd claimed to be hurt by my fall. The incident was front-page news for seven days in New England, and I was treated as a criminal by the media.

The only thing I can say now is if I did hurt someone, I would take full responsibility. But I know in my heart I didn't hurt anyone.

I did apologize to my teammates, coaches, and community for my poor choice.

It was unwise for an NFL quarterback to jump off a stage into a crowd. I didn't break any laws, and it wasn't immoral, but I still didn't think about the consequences. Sometimes choices we make don't seem dumb at the time, but they are. You can be sure I won't make that mistake again.

"The probability of someone watching you is directly proportional to the stupidity of your actions."

39

The support of Maura, my family, and friends—the people who know me best—has helped me through life's low points.

The birth of my son, Stu McQueen, was one of my all-time highlights. Now that I have a son, my decisions are more important than ever, because they affect Stu. Becoming a parent changes the way you look at things. Everything on my Top 20 List, after God, moved down a notch.

Like millions of others who have a child "on loan," now it's Maura's and my turn to be the life teachers. I could win 10 Super Bowls, but if I do not succeed as a parent I would consider myself a failure.

Being a parent has taught me to appreciate all the things my parents did for me. Be sure to thank your parents for what they've done for you.

Most of all, remember the best anyone can do, guided by priorities day by day, is to try and make the right call.

Drew with his parents.

"To understand your parents' love, you must raise children yourself."